CW01663931

In Search of Serenity

~

A collection of poems and other Spirit Teachings

by

Ann E. Harrison

published by

Saturday Night Press Publications
England.
snppbooks@gmail.com
www.snppbooks.com

ISBN 978-1-908421-37-1

www.snppbooks.com

Photograph of Iris and cover design by Ann Harrison, May 2020

Dedicated to

the friends on this and the 'other' side of life
who have helped me find my Way.
and
in memory of my two wonderful men
Norman Ellis and Tom Harrison

Contents

"Live life that the fear of death can never enter your heart. Trouble no one about their religion; respect others in their view and demand that they respect yours.

Love your life, perfect your life, and beautify all things in your life. Seek to make your life long and its purpose in the service of your people... Always give a word or salute of greeting when meeting or passing a friend, even a stranger when in a lonely place. Show respect to all people and grovel to none. When you arise in the morning give thanks for the food and for the joy of living. If you see no reason for giving thanks, the fault lies only in yourself... Abuse no one and no thing... When it comes your time to die, be not like those whose hearts are filled with the fear of death, so that when their time comes they weep and pray for a little more time to live their lives over again in a different way. Sing your death song and die like a hero going home."

Tecumseh, Chief (Crouching Tiger) of the
Shawnee nation (1768 -1813)*

*From an English language newspaper article in Spain, May 2010. Written by Bernie Comaskey & printed with the permission of Westmeath Examiner. ~ My thanks.

Introduction

In late 1989 when my husband was told he was terminally ill, he said to me "What am I going to do without you?" My reply was "But I'm the one who has to stay here." Until that moment we hadn't really given a thought to whether or not there was an afterlife nor did we in the following weeks. However, within a month of his 'death' in June 1990, he was back, at Morley Spiritualist church, near Leeds, communicating through a medium from Huddersfield during the tea session after an Open Circle. I still have no idea who this medium was. He was most insistent that the lady to whom the medium was speaking knew his sister. The evidence that followed made her realise that she did. The message that the pain had gone was relayed to his sister, Bess, and when she told me my reaction was "When can I come?" It seemed a perfectly natural response, which is how it should be.

The FIVE weeks I had to wait was an eternity. My visit to Morley church didn't give me contact with him but it whetted my appetite. The following weekend found me at a church in Hull, where I not only met people I already knew, but I felt had come home. The second week, at the end of the service as they announced the speakers for the following weekend, a voice inside my head kept repeating "Pat'll have it." That was one of the mediums coming from Sheffield to take the service the following Saturday. Panic! How could I rearrange family commitments? It was 'managed' and the following Saturday I had the most conclusive evidence and a joyous reunion with my darling man.

Three months later I was invited to sit with the church healing group and that was when my understanding and development began and the writing started to flow. I have struggled since young to write even poor verse but now I would feel impelled to find a pen and the words would pour out. If I interfered they would stop.

I would apologise, cross out the bit I had put in, and they would continue. Some of the longer poems came when I would ask for a reading for the Sunday evening service, others would come during meditation. I know that it is not great poetry, but I hope that those which helped me express the physical loss I felt will help others. For although we may know that our 'dead' are safe and perhaps we talk on the 'telephone', we still need to grieve - not for them, but for our own loss. The writings mirror, too, my search for answers and a deeper peace of heart and mind.

By the end of 1991 I was persuaded to put some of the pieces into book form. I printed it myself and sold it for church funds. More pieces came and I reworked the original edition adding the later writings and others which I had felt earlier were too personal. I put them in a larger format with, in some cases, short introductions, plus my ink sketches of flowers I love. (My later drawings appear different as they were originally ink and colour.)

As I learned more of Spiritual/Psychic Awareness and trusted the voice more, not only did poems come in for Sunday Evening services but other voices gave pieces for guidance. Occasionally they added humorous touches - just to see if I would record it, I suppose.

In 1994-95 my life took a dramatic change, and as I transformed from Ann Ellis into Ann Harrison so too did the voices that I heard and 'felt' for my writings. The gentle feminine voice I had felt for many of the rhyming poems left me and now there was a stronger influence. Now the words that came were often in response to a situation or a word and at times most unexpected. Sometimes it came as a "consideration" or "play" on words. Sometimes it was as advice for someone, but always there was depth to the thought in what was given. As there is such a change in "Voice" I have put these later ones in a separate section.

I hope that you enjoy reading and perhaps using them.

Ann Ellis Harrison
April 2020.

UNIVERSAL ENERGY

The Laws of Physics state
that energy cannot be destroyed -
only changed.
And every atom of our bodies is that
which cannot be destroyed -
only recycled
within the ever-changing universe.

So, when the physical form returns
to the earth from whence it came;
dust to dust, ashes to ashes;
where is the energy that was life,
the uniqueness that was you?

Was it all just for this -
the loving and the learning,
the laughter and the tears,
to be only a memory
on the wind?

A LIFE LOST

Where is that energy we all admired
That precious vital spark of Life?
How could a heart that beat so strong
be stilled?
Where has that spirit gone?
For energy cannot be destroyed.

A Wednesday's child you sure were born.
A life of woe you knew.
A life of pain and bitterness
was hidden inside of you.
To friends you showed a brighter side,
the hurt was known by few.
You could not forgive and let it go
and the pain at last broke through.

We fought and lost the battle for life.
But was it lost
or have you won?
Did you learn the lessons
you came to learn?
Was your earthly life 'well done'?

THE KNOWING

By the way I'm never lonely,
By the way my heart will pound,
By the way I feel you're close to me
I know you're still around.

You say, I never talk much.
I didn't when you were here.
We never seemed to need it;
It was enough just being there.

Living with you, Love, was easy.
There was always so much to do.
As for learning and forming opinions,
I left all the thinking to you.

I never wanted to lose you,
Though we knew that you'd be first to go.
I was lost when I thought that you'd left me
But you're here -
and I'm ready to grow.

* * * * *

THE VOICE OF GOD

In quietness you'll hear my voice,
In peace you'll feel me near,
but your days you spend
in bustle and noise
rushing from
there to here.
Why don't
you
stop
sit,
take time.
All will be done
that needs to be done,
if in quietness you will hear
and in peace you feel me near.

THE ANSWER

This was written at one of my 'lowest' points, eight months after my husband's passing. I did not realise at the time how easy it was to communicate, if you trusted. The first three verses came in the space of 20 minutes on a Saturday evening after my return from a service but on reading it on the Sunday morning I said "Yes, but ..." and the other half flowed. The last two verses came through with such a force it was as though God Himself was speaking. I had no idea then of how much my life would be changed and the work I would be doing but I'm loving every minute of it.

They say 'death is nothing at all'
Just a step to a far brighter day
They say that you're close, oh so near,
That you're only a whisper away.
But my heart aches so sorely now
That I can't put my arms around you.
I can talk to you love any time
But when will an answer come through?

Patience you tell me, just wait,
The months will pass fleetingly by.
You are walking a strange new path.
You ask where you're going and why.
We are all waiting to guide you;
To help you and mark out your way.
You'll need a calm heart and strong nerve
To follow this different way.

We're waiting, my dear one, we're waiting
Until you are ready to start;
Until with the others we've chosen,
You can work and play a full part.
Then onward together we'll travel.
You will see beyond the fine veil,
And the Peace which passeth all knowing,
Over unreasoning doubt will prevail.

But what of those not ready to travel
for whom the days drag on and on,
When the one that they spent
their whole life with,
the one that they loved so is gone.
the one that they laughed with and leaned on,
the one that shared the downs too,
the one that to them now is - dead.
What then, O God, do they do?

Call on My Name, child, and mean it;
Remind them they call not in vain.
From the depths of despair and in anguish
Remember how you called My Name.

Your guardian angel is with you,
Your 'lost' family and friends all around.
Just send out your love and you'll find them
And My Peace
in your heart - will abound.

OPEN MY EYES ....

These were the opening words of the first hymn I heard when very new to the idea, I went to a Spiritualist church in Hull. The words embodied the craving I had for spiritual knowledge. These verses developed from my love of that inspiring hymn.

"Open my eyes that I might see"
Is how I pray each night to thee.
Grant I may hear what thou wouldst speak
As truth and light from thee I seek.

May thy great Love forever flow,
As we in consciousness, slowly grow,
That the Spark Divine within us all
Responds more surely at thy call.

Open my eyes that I may see
My fellow who has need of me,
That I may serve our God above
By helping those in need of Love.

May thy pure Light forever be
There for those who would truly see.
O, Spark Divine, within my heart
Ignite the flame so I may start!

WHERE?

I suppose most people wonder whether or not they have lived here before and have they special lessons to learn whilst here. I certainly have often wondered about these matters.

Where am I going?
Where have I been?
What is my purpose
Upon this earth's plane?

No-one can answer,
Until I return,
Whether my journey
Was not all in vain.

Where am I going?
How far have I come?
The source of my quest
Is beyond the dark veil.

So live for the day!
Give it the best that you can.
All the 'Well I was going to's,'
Cut no ice when you've gone.

And perhaps back you may journey,
To see if you can
Get a better result
When you sit Life's exam.

CALLED

Who was it called in the dead of night?
So clearly called my name?
I ran to my love,
was he ill or in pain?
But no, he still quietly lay.

Back to my bed I went
puzzled,
Who could have called
so plain?
And just as I was dozing off,
there it came again!
'I'm coming,' I called,
'I'm coming.'
a reassuring word
and went again to his bedside,
but no he hadn't stirred.

The voice had been so firm,
so clear,
Was it just inside my head?
Weary now at 2 a.m.
I climbed back into bed.

Deep in sleep, again it came.
This time I lay quite still
to see if he really needed me,
was he dreaming
or feeling ill?

No sound I heard
from the room below.
'It's like Samuel.' I mused
but hadn't the sense
to do as he did and say,
'Speak, Lord,
I'm ready to be used.'

Baffled, I settled myself for sleep
and slept
till the light brought day

But in daylight
there was still no answer
to who called
in so urgent a way.

Slowly the days crept into weeks
and my loved one sickened and failed.
Never again did I hear the sound
of that someone calling my name.

Now alone and racked with grief
I heard my mother call.
I woke with a start,
a child once more
but there was nobody with me
at all!

One day, when the sorrow was hard to bear
And the tears flowed on for hours,
I called out
'GOD - Somebody - Help!'
And felt -
'Go work 'mongst your flowers!'

Slowly a peace crept over me
and calm in my heart was restored
as I worked in our garden
all summer through
I strengthened my trust in the Lord.

I've God's peace in my heart now,
a lot of the time
although tears do come, now and then,
but I know if I hear
that strong voice
in the night,
I'll say 'Speak now, Lord,
and forever - Amen!'

And one day,
if I learn to listen and watch,
I will talk with my loved one, again.

JUST A THOUGHT...

The scientists all tell us
that energy cannot be destroyed,
only changed.
That every atom of our bodies is
that which cannot be destroyed,
only recycled.
Our very thoughts, for good or bad,
are energy and cannot,
once set free,
be, like faulty goods, recalled
to be destroyed!

Think on!

THE LOVE WITHIN

His Love is closer than a second skin
For that love wells from deep within.
The heart is not just flesh and blood
It really has that sense for good.

It's not just our brain that leads the way
That makes decisions from day to day.
The life force from whence we all began
Will hold the choice to do good for Man.

The spark of God within your soul
May place you in a healer's role
And bring forth the kinder side of you
To consider others in the things you do.

Please listen to that voice within
It's not just keeping us from sin.
Find time to sit and quiet be
And hopefully you'll find the key -

To who you are and why you're here
And for heaven's sake,
it's not just for the beer!

* * * * *

A PRAYER FOR DIRECTION

O Lord who has created a place
for everything
and everything for a purpose.
May we find our place and purpose
in this earthly life,
that we grow daily in Thy Image
And by our example
draw others to your Light.
Amen

A SONG OF HARMONY

After listening to a boys' choir singing the original words of the New Seekers' song I could not get the tune out of my head and suddenly there were these words.

I'd like to teach the world to sing
a song of harmony,
that if we love our Father God
the world could better be.
His Love is great, it covers all.
He loves both great and small
And if you're hurt or suffering
He loves you most of all.

His Way is Love, and Truth and Light,
Just spread it all around
And soon you'll find your spirits lift you
right up off the ground
His Light is bright, through darkest night
He shows the way to go.
So lift your heart towards that light
And you will find it so.

His Truth is there for all to see;
'Twas written long ago,
Just love all men as you love him
While on your path you go.
His rules are few, remember them.
Love God and all men too
And see how bright your light can shine
For those who follow you.

THE MASTERMIND

When you look around you
at the wonders you can see,
there has to be a mastermind,
there simply has to be!

When you think of how the tides come in,
pulled by the moon
to and fro,
and the deep seas carry tiny shells
to Herm from Mexico;
That an elephant knows
how big to grow,
and a mouse that it must stay small
The scientists say
"It's all in the genes."
But HOW
do the genes know it all?

A cheetah's as fast as
the weakest gazelle,
the wings of an owl make no beat,
and giraffes have a neck
that is just so long -
to reach the leaves that they eat.

If you think how our nerves
react, so swift -
in the twinkling of an eye;
that blood carries
food and oxygen,
and there are tears
when we need to cry.

There has to be a Mastermind
behind it all you see
and I think it's not just
'out there'
but in the Heart of you and me !

• *(Herm is one of the Channel Islands.)*

HOW DO YOU USE YOUR POWER?

Occasionally between the rhyming poems would come a teaching from Spirit. This is one such.

You have the ability to use your power
to work for world good
But so often ego comes into it
and as the power centre is in the throat
we find that sore throats develop,
when trying to exert power over others.

You need to be hooked to a higher level
to use power wisely,
and rely on - 'Thy will not mine, Lord.'
Remember God is not mocked.

If you are in a quandary
as to where to channel your energies
and feel pressure is constantly being put on you
to help Africa or other parts of the world,
consider -
Is the emotional battle in the trauma of inner-city life
any less destructive than the starvation of the physical body
in other countries?
It is your responsibility to use your power rightly
and humbly accept what is shown to you as your path.

We have great concern also for the planet itself.
It needs our healing.
You are breathing in rubbish in the air,
but work is constantly being done
on channelling energies for good along the Leys.

The main concern is that you use wisely -
and to the utmost,
the gifts you have been given,
hooked in always,
to the supra-conscious -

The Highest Mind.

A PRAYER FOR PEACE

This poem was written in January '91, just before the Gulf War, after watching a TV programme about the American Indians and the centenary ceremony that had been held at Wounded Knee in December 1990.
Harry Charger, of Sans Arc Sioux, describing how he had stood beside the Keeper of the Pipe, said "We prayed, he also prayed, prayed for peace – not world peace – but peace within himself, and with peace, forgiveness comes."

He murmured a prayer for peace
they said
as he stood beside the grave.
A quiet, inward prayer for peace
in memory of the brave.
It wasn't a big prayer -
for peace throughout the world.
No.
Just a little prayer
for peace within himself
and the man next to him.
For with that peace,
within one's self,
comes forgiveness for a wrong done,
and from that peace
comes love and respect
for man,
regardless of what he's become.
And as this peace spreads
from man to man,
with respect for culture and creed,
so love can spread
throughout the world
and replace cruel war and greed.
So say that prayer within yourself,
for the peace in you
and your friend,
That the peace he asked for
at Wounded Knee
may spread through the world –
without end.

SPRING

This the first mild day of March,
the great poet said so long ago,
and this is just one such as that.

Under a clean blue sky
the sun has opened the gentle crocus
in a mat of fragile
mauve and gold.
And the air is alive with the hum
of hungry bees.

Small and brown
or fat and furry
they hurry from flower to flower
to gather in what bounty they can
on the still, short afternoon,
as a ladybird warms itself
on an aromatic leaf of Bay.

So, from my task of tidying away
the past glories of last summer,
I'll take time to stand,
alone,
and watch and pray
that winter has passed,
and, as the cycle of life begins again
in the earth,
so will it, in my heart.

THOUGHTS

The thoughts that carry us along
May spring from deep within,
The thoughts that well from our soul's depths
Are surely born of Him.
We know not how those thoughts might come
Or where their path will lead,
But all true thoughts are sent from Him.
He plants the Holy Seed.

Our soul can only show the way
If we will listen hard,
For if we wish to use free will
Our way will not be barred,
But if to God our life we give
Then we will see the way,
It may not be what we would wish
And we still can have our say.

But surely then as we progress
The light will lead us back
And when we ask to know our God
There's nothing we will lack.
So we'll go ever onward
Towards our heavenly home,
Where we will blend together
In his pure blessed zone.

For all true thoughts come straight from Him,
And back to Him they fly,
For hearts attuned down here on earth
Form a bridge to those on high.
So keep your thoughts tuned in to God,
How ever dull the task,
And if you ever need some help
You only have to ask!

LOVE YOUR MOTHER ...

The world is a beautiful place,
All that everyone wants it to be,
From the valleys to peaks and high meadows,
From the deserts to jungle and sea.

It's all that mankind ever wished for
To give him the food that he needs.
Each part in a delicate balance
With seasons for blossom and seed.

The Guardians of Earth are so sad now.
Man's greed is destroying their charge;
Ever mining and spraying and dumping
And profit's the word, by and large.

We know that you all want home comforts
And do like a change now and then
But think now - before you go dump it,
Can it be used by less fortunate men?

Can the metal, the glass and the plastic,
Made by boring in to the Earth's heart,
Be collected and cleaned and reprocessed?
It can, if you'll all play a part.

Can the forest be saved from destruction,
And the desert be fertile once more?
Can the fish have clean water to swim in?
Yes, but you'll have to work fast - that's for sure!

For your bones they are made from her minerals
And her plants make the air that you breathe.
You'll find that you can't live without her
And your children will have the same need.

But you'll need to voice your opinions,
And start making the effort also,
For remember from tiny beginnings
The wonderful oak trees will grow.

Come pitch in now - all together.
How much is a good mother worth?
She's fed you and clothed and protected,
Start giving *Love* back to the Earth.

A GREATER UNDERSTANDING

I wish to speak of Greater Understanding.
The continuity of souls and greater understanding
are beyond
and above our belief.
The Universe is limited only by our horizons.
As we progress as a soul
the horizons would seemingly be endless.
Therefore limit not yourself.

"My eyes are dim I cannot see
I have not brought my specs with me."
as they sing
- we laugh!

We say "Judge not that ye be not judged."
For who are we to say that everyone else is wrong?
We know not where the other is along the path.
We know not what tests or restrictions
are placed upon the Soul for this life.

Great Buddha stressed -
"Because his way is different
does not signify it is wrong -
it is simply different."
There are many paths to the Godhead.
For as the Christ force said
"In my father's house there are many mansions."

Many evenings have been spent discussing this
and in that house -
there are very many mansions
and there is understanding for everybody.

NOT SEALING WAX

Once again I come my friends,
To talk of many things,
Not shoes, nor ships, nor sealing wax.
not cabbages, nor kings.
But finer higher things than these
That we search for all along,
The knowledge that we are of God;
To him we all belong.

His love for us is deep and sure,
So held within our soul
Is a sureness that there's something more
Than the earth-bound life we know.

Each man may take a different path
As his way to God he finds
But remember God's not just in church,
He's also in our minds!

To know and keep ourselves in love
Is the only way to go
And so - we grow.
Not as a plant will grow,
Quickly fading to shed its seed
But blossoming ever beautiful -
Don't be a pernicious weed.

Where we will go, what we will do
May not be very grand
But to live this earthly life,
Is how it all was planned.

Not to search for far off mountains,
Or some valley, strange and deep
But here at home our work is done
In promises we keep.
In caring for our families
And those friends we see each day
And - if there's love left over
Then send it on its way-

To help in other lands,
So those who feel the call
May have the strength to take them
Where there's the greatest need of all.

But if you're wondering why
You don't feel the need to roam.
It is because you're needed,
Most of all, right here - at home.

REMEMBERING

In prayer, Dear Lord, we ask for peace
And thoughts of Love abound
But do we always remember this
When we deal with the man on the ground?

In prayer, Dear Lord, we send out thoughts
to heal all manner of ill,
But do we always remember to add
Not mine, O Lord, but Thy Will?

In prayer, Dear Lord, we seek to know
What you would have us do,
But do we always listen, Lord,
When you send the answer through?

In prayer, Dear Lord, we humbly beg,
Grant us Your Will to know.
Help us to love, on earth, as above,
And nearer to you may we grow.

Amen.

THE TRUMPET CALL

Above us and below us
And on every side beset
Are the trials and tribulations
That as man we can't forget.

But in glorious array,
Waits the army of the Lord
They are ready there to help us,
Just waiting for the word.

The word for which they're waiting
Transcends all thought above;
A word of true compassion,
The trumpet call is Love.

Misunderstood and misconstrued,
We cage that glorious word.
In narrow confines pin it down,
Forget Love's like a bird.

A bird that knows no boundaries,
That soars all earth above;
And so, like lark ascending,
Will soar our prayers of Love.

In colours bright, set free the thought
To wing all earth around,
To lift the heart of each soul touched,
So their love can swell the sound.

For then in peace and harmony
The balance we restore.
And the army of the Lord has WON,
For it never goes to war.

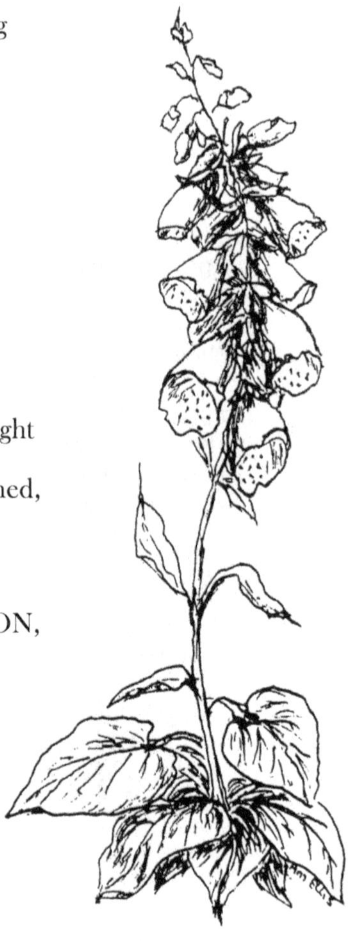

THE WATERS OF TIME

The waters of time flow ever on
and our memories dim
and details fade
but thoughts of love - live
when once released.
Their power builds the future path of hope.

Light, however faint, glows in faces once
the spark is struck
and with gentle fanning may ignite a fire.
But protect it well
lest gales of discouragement or derision
snuff out the wavering spark.

Nurture the new,
encompass the frail,
enfold the lonely heart -
And give just thought to life
As the waters of time flow on.

THE AWAKENING

These verses came in response to a wish to help a young woman who came to the church because she had just started 'hearing voices' (particularly when she was doing the washing-up!) to reassure her that it was all quite natural and a wonderful gift which she could use.

It's another step along the way,
The way you have to go.
Just another step along the way,
And a little more you'll know.
You think that there's a lot to learn,
How much you'll never know.
Just take in what you can for now,
As on the way you go.

You'll sit and try so hard to reach
The voices that you hear
And yet by keeping, oh, so still,
You'll learn when they are near.
You dare not tell your kith and kin
What happens when no-one's near.
They'd say 'You're going round the bend.'
If you spoke of the things that you hear.

But do not be afraid to speak
To us of the sounds that you heard.
We know exactly what you mean
And we'll answer, 'Don't be scared.
The voices don't mean you're going mad;
Remember how Samuel heard.
They're messages from the 'other' side,
From a real, yet invisible world.'

So keep your trust in what you hear
And your gift will surely grow
To help all those who turn to you
When life's sorrows lay them low.

May God's Love and Truth
be with you always.

THANKSGIVING

Thank you, God, for the privilege
Of sitting here bathed in your Love,
For having the chance to say 'Thank you'
For the blessings you send from above.

We sit here in the hope of some contact
With someone far wiser than we.
That with their help and their guidance
Greater use in the world we will be.

We send out our peace and our love now,
Thou knowst where best they'll be used,
It may be for nothing dramatic,
Just some help for a soul that's abused.

So we thank you, God for the privilege,
Of being with those of like mind;
For having the chance to say 'Thank you,'
For the wonderful peace that we find.

INVOCATION OF THE LIGHT

One December a group of us who met to read and discuss Spiritual books and ideas, decided, as it was approaching the Solstice, to put together some readings and songs based on the theme of light.
It was my task to put all the pieces into a form which could be used as a service and this was the poem 'given' to me to close the miscellany.

Incandescent Spirit of the Flame,
The form within the Light,
May we know the Love you bring
Will lead us to Day from Night.

Living flame of Light and Life,
As unto you we turn,
Ignite the spark within our hearts
And ever let it burn.

To burn and yet not be consumed,
As things material are.
But burn with Love, our spirit fired,
A shining brand new star.

A new star in the firmament
Like the pole star, there to guide,
Or even if I'm, oh so small,
Let me not my candle hide.

For one candle to a room of light
It matters not one jot
But in the darkness we can see
What earlier we could not.

Incandescent Spirit of the Flame
Keep us ever in your sight,
So the soul that walks in Darkness now
May find that gleam of Light.

THE FIRST CHRISTMAS AFTER ....

Christmas 1994 saw me writing cards and letters to several of my friends and family who had lost someone very dear to them during the year. Christmas is very much a family time and you notice the loss even more keenly. I thought back to my own 'First' Christmas and my new knowledge.

This year Christmas is - different,
the lights and the music are
just as insistent -
but smiles fade as we miss them.
Their life's burden is eased
and sorrow lifted
in the soul's release,
to be reborn in perfect peace,
but we miss them.

Though they're often here around us
we just can't seem to see.
It really is frustrating.
This is not how it should be.

They want to tell us of the wonder
and the beauty in their land;
that is further than Australia
yet right here so close at hand;
of the light, the peace, the colours,
the freedom from all pain,
the wholeness and the loving -
and that they miss us - just the same.

Perhaps, one day, we'll hear them
in the stillness of our minds
and the love that is within us
will be theirs again - alive.

So try smiling, while remembering
all the lovely happy times,
and be glad that you had someone
whose departing made you sad.
Then, the shiver that goes through you
or the warmth that wraps you round
may be a hug from them, for Christmas,
to say, 'We're still around.'

A PRAYER FOR THF EARTH

Lord of air and earth,
of fire and water,
true elements of your
boundless Love.
From these you formed
the whole world order–
the rock beneath, the bird above.

May the Breath of God be with us
when the gentle breezes blow,
And the fire of transformation
make the heart within us glow.
For our earth is all sustaining
feeding great and small alike,
and the water is your blessing,
flowing as the blood of life.

May we just one of your creations
be mindful of
the wondrous whole
and in our daily thoughts
and actions
make loving care for all
our goal.

A BLESSING

The Peace that passeth all understanding
Is with you and in you, tonight.
The Peace that all your hearts are demanding
Is yours, if you trust a-right.

The Love that gives of itself, unceasing,
Is yours, my dears, by right.
The Love that you give to others, unstinting,
Is most blessed in his sight.

The Wisdom which you seek, unfailing,
Is yours, when you walk in light.
The wisdom imparted to another
Is leading the world to light.

God Bless you, my children.

* * * * *

A PRAYER FOR WISDOM

Father make me a vessel
filled with your wisdom
so that I may give
to those
who
thirst
and they will
Know your Light.

Amen

IN SEARCH OF SERENITY

Calm as a swan on sun-dappled pool
at peace with the world,
life I savour,
But knowing how way leads on to way
let my trust in Your Love
never waver.

With one thrust of a powerful foot
from below
the swan glides
o'er the mirror-like stream.
May Your power be likewise
that thrust in my life
that I glide like the swan,
so serene.

May the petty emotions
that ruffle the calm,
in the undertow be swept to the bottom,
and the hurts and the knocks
I have met with till now,
be submerged in the depths
and forgotten.

It is easier to glide along with the stream
than to paddle so hard 'gainst its flow.
Much harder the journey
'gainst the tide of mankind
to the source of all being, you know.

When, with rapids and rocks,
further progress is blocked
may I call on Your help from above,
and like the swan -
spread my wings,
and be borne on Your wind,
to the source of my being -
Your Love.

I loved watching the swans on our village pond. This poem described what was going on in my life at the time. Only later did I discover the esoteric meaning. I'm working on living up to it! The Swan has long been used as a symbol for spiritual power and purity; having the power to overcome evil.

THE DREAM

Today, before the morn
Had begun
I dreamed of a song
that needed to be sung.
I dreamed of a hope
that once in the heart
might lie -
unborn
like the song to be sung.

I dreamed of a choice
that needed to be made
before the hope could grow
and the song be sung.
I dreamed of a life
that could waste away
if all I did was dream all day.

With this song in my heart
I woke to the day
saying - NOW -
is the choice to be made;
to work, really work
in the way that I should
so the notes of the song
never fade:
so the hopes and the dreams
may steadily grow
till they blossom and fruit on my tree;
and the light and the peace
that I feel deep within,
soon everyone will share with me.

May the light and the love
of the Peace of the World
be with you.

A CHANGE OF VOICE

More Thoughts, Writings and Teachings given and inspired by Spirit Teachers

As the Millenium and the 'Dawn of a New Age' approached so the feelings deepened and at times became abstract, but they touch the core. Just occasionally, as before it, was my own soul speaking but many times the voice of a Higher Soul is evident in the words I was given to write.

I hope that you can appreciate the thoughts and emotions behind these pieces.

A NEW BEGINNING

Beginning again,
Starting anew
Building the pattern
This time, without you
Beginning to live
Starting again
But the pieces don't fit
the way that they did
I'm not the old me -
I'm not starting again
I'm -
  beginning anew!

ADVICE FROM SPIRIT

During a Seminar at Cober Hill in North Yorkshire, as we sat in a period of Contemplation, this advice given to me for a young man in the group – but it could apply to you!

Problems are of your own making
The way you approach your life
stops you from making progress
in any new direction
and many of the old directions have become cul-de-sacs.

So 'back-up' and get the map out.
It is not a maze but a pathway.
You are not meant to go down blind alleys.
They only delay the discovery of the inevitable beauty,
this builds up frustrations within you and stifles the mental
and, eventually, the physical body.

Give yourself permission to BE.

Give yourself permission to be rid of ....

Give yourself permission to receive new stimulation, just like the
pot plants that need that dose of Phostrogen or BabyBio
if their life is not to lose its colour and strength.

And thank God for your being –
Free to explore
and accepting your new pathway forward.

RANDOM THOUGHTS

When during a mediumship development class I was asked to think of a word, out of the blue came this – and as I sat quietly later, in came these thoughts.

Tangent

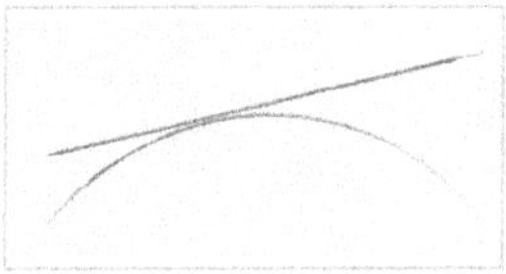

A straight line - a curve - a surface that meets a curve at a point
but does not intersect it
- at a tangent - diverge from a previous course ...
- perhaps of thinking ...

An effect on someone's life - that is changed for ever
- however great or small.

Intuition - a sudden impulse to make that change -
GO off at a tangent...

The ancient Pythagorean system
of taking numbers for letters gives us -
2,1,5,7,5,5,2 = 27 = 9 - the universal number
containing all human emotion and experience
- and marks the end of a cycle -

A time to pick up the loose ends and get ready for the future -

And go off at a tangent for further growth -
for material gain or consciousness?

"Two roads diverged in a yellow wood
and I took the one less travelled by..."*

* *Two lines from my favourite poem by Robert Frost.*

PLAISIR D'AMOUR

While waiting for a lecture to start at a Linwood Fellowship weekend in 1999, John, one of the delegates, was playing the piano. He started to play 'Plaisir d'amour' and as I listened, I felt compelled to write. (I later performed it, together with John playing the tune, at the end of conference concert).

Plaisir d'amour
The pleasure - the joyful pleasure of love,
 - of loving.
The giving of the light of the heart.
The overwhelming stirring of emotion
from within,
as one stranger, meeting a friend - as yet unknown
unintroduced - is introduced:
unrecognised before,
in the blending of the energies
becomes now
a shared experience
a con-fidence -
a welcoming
of knowing each other a-new.
For the energies are not unfamiliar
once we overcome the diffidence
of introduction
and the enjoyable pleasure
of meeting these - old friends
is a true -
Plaisir d'amour!

THOUGHTS ON SPIRIT AND ANGELS

At the end of a short meditation during another weekend with others 'of like mind', we were asked to give the word which surfaced in our minds the moment the tutor came to us. When the list was completed we were asked to link back into our minds and use as many of those eleven words as possible to build an inspirational text. This is what came into my mind in seconds. (the words we gave are shown in heavy type.)

Spirit

The **I am** of the Universe
The **inspiration** of **stardust**
Without and **within**
Having **trust** in the voice of the Spirit -
Without and **within,**
As **spouts** of **water** - **love** pours
And **we** add our **teardrops**
Of remorse and compassion.

We repeated the exercise and eleven new words were given by the students. These lines came into my mind instantly.

A Philosophy of Angels

They - the energy of **light**
Behind, beneath all that we do
 - and feel,
if we allow that **ethereal beauty**
To penetrate the earthly cares:
holding us **up** through all
the blockages of life -
the **waters** of sorrow-
Leading us with **love,**
Lighting our **pathway**
To an ever-**shining day.**

IT ALL DEPENDS

It all depends on what you think is important, as your life can depend upon it and you may come to be dependent on it too.

The waves of dependency may be overwhelming without the knowledge that there is only one thing that you can depend on with absolute certainty and that is the dependability of God and his Love.

You are part of the whole creation, a tiny dependent cell in the whole body of creation. You cannot exist without it - but it can exist without you. You depend on it for the air that you breathe, the food that you eat and the water that you drink.

It is no good looking to other planets or space for somewhere else to live because only here are the elements you depend on to survive. Yes, they can be transported to a base station, but wherever you are, you are dependent on others.

Even in that dependent state there are others who are dependent upon you - so how good is your dependability?

How dependable are you in support of those dependent on you?

For your praise or condemnation of an idea, a plan, can raise them up or crush them totally.

You have a great responsibility to those dependent on you, who look to you for sustenance. An ill-considered remark may send them off on a wrong track or bring to an end a promising dream.

You are not the prefect judge of all things but as a dependable being, in touch with your creator, you can do the best you are capable of by sometimes just saying -

"It all depends on what you want from this

- on what you want to do with this,

- on where you intend your path to be."

In teaching considered opinion, you make those dependants - independent. As their own self grows so those others, back down the track, can come to depend on them and their dependable spirit.

But remember there is always that Infinite Dependable Being from whom all reliance comes, and on whom we all depend at sometime, even those who don't believe in him when all else become undependable.

So depending on where you are going and what you intend to do at this stage of your journey - it all depends on you!

* * * * *

WHO YOU ARE

'Bend me, shake me' says the song but -
Once you learn who you are
Nothing and nobody can break your will.
Your knowledge then surpasses
all that you have ever learned.
The overwhelming evidence
of the beauty of life
Presses in upon you,
and joy pours from you
You are - you always will be
the most Wonderful being.
You will protect and defend all,
And nothing will shake you.

YOU CHOOSE!

How often do we hear that word when someone doesn't want to make the decision? And so pushes the decision on to you - when you had given them the choice because you hadn't wanted to choose either, knowing that decision needed to be equally arrived at.

In surrendering our preference to another may give rise to unjust accusations of having some unwanted choice foisted upon us at any time in the future - if things don't go right.

And how often do we give up our right to choose by not making it known what we would like?

Unless of course we choose to give it away.

A wise old man, who appeared to be extremely put-upon by others who seemed to be taking advantage of him, and using him, replied that he was not being taken advantage of, because he was choosing to allow it.

We are told that this is the only planet of free will—where we can plan our own path, make our own choices—right or wrong and if it is 'wrong' we learn by those mistakes. And usually the circumstances of the lesson are repeated in some other situation for us to deal with again, until we learn which choice to make.

Sometimes, if we choose what we believe is right for us - perhaps for us the easiest way - we then find ourselves being guided back to what we are supposed to be doing. We can fight that and maybe we can have an easy life - perhaps we can have a reasonably happy life, but somehow we never feel fulfilled.

OR we can choose to follow a more difficult path that, with support from all those unseen friends, we can say in the end "I've done my best" and feel a sense of satisfaction.

All from having had the right to choose!

SYNCHRONICITY

The moments when worlds collide
Seemingly at Random -
As our thoughts, our actions, are mirrored
by an unknown intrusion from somewhere
beyond -
and in that second
the meeting takes on a special significance.
A memory is ignited and love lit.
Which came first
the distant act or ours?
Who can say -
but the action of the collision implies
harmony -
and reassurance that what we do
is met with approval.
We are where we should be -
And all's well in our world.

ACOUSTICS

These words were received, unbidden, during the ITC conference in Vigo, N-W Spain in 2004. That weekend Presentations were given in three languages, so simultaneous translation via headphones was provided if required.

Sound – spaces that move with the waves allowing the molecules to reach the apparatus.
You appreciate the sound that falls gently on the ear
and pleasantly affects the mind with its pitch and its cadence.
You have learned to switch off to familiar unbidden sounds
but will accept, albeit unwillingly,
the soul sound when in an unfamiliar way
it is presented to you.
We work endlessly with effort to bring to you these sounds
and awaken the sense that you may hear
in waking state the voice you are familiar with,
not just bells and shouts,
but the flow of speech we can transmit as thought flow.
We appreciate that this will take further sleep state work.
In joyous communication

We come, you know not when....

We come, you wait.....

WHEN WILL THEY EVER LEARN!!

These thoughts were also received during a non-English very technical presentation which was beyond me, in Vigo – 24th April 2004.

What is this world if full of care we have no time to . . . think on other ways, approaches and consider the ideas, thoughts and research of others which until now has not concerned nor interested us.

We need to follow where the path leads and a conjunction of other ways gives us the opportunity to stretch not only the imagination but, hopefully our path, to include others.

Synchronicity of paths and ideas pushes forward the barriers that have previously divided us.

For are we not all working to one end? That of enabling total communication between all levels without the need for divisive language.

If only we were able to pass ideas by picture or emotional thoughts as through the form of thought in the discarnate world. We know that this will not take place, for the tribes and races of the earth cling too ferociously to their individuality; that their way should not be thought to be less than another's by relinquishing it. The Tower of Babel was supposedly created to divide man, and the suppression of the psychic sense has further frustrated international communication.

Man becomes much more adept at confusing what should be a simple acceptance of the efforts we make to communicate with the scientific advances that they "discover". We have worked hard along with them to support these advances but instead of seeing that they support our efforts, they often use them to discredit the evidence.

When, when, when will they ever learn!!

IN THOUGHT

While I contemplate the beauty of my world
I thank God for the gifts of sight and sound.
I see the wild cyclamen at my step,
The winter visitor returning to my table
for his sweet crumbs,
And I thank God for these pleasures.

As I hear the soft notes of a piano
repeating a gentle melody,
I thank God for those who write these notes,
the wizards who devise the systems to play them,
And the engineers who make the power for them possible,

And I thank God for my world
For many do not know these pleasures.

So I take time to sit and think of them
And ask that their pleasures may be as sweet to them
as mine are
And I thank God.

AN ESSENTIAL FOR HUMANITY

During JV Trust week, at Stansted Hall, August 2010, I worked with Gerard Smith on Inspirational thought and writing. One 'Homework' was to consider what we thought was the most essential thing for humanity. As I sat on my bed that night to consider this, these words came as strong as a heard voice.

Is there one thing which is essential for all aspects of life -
for earth - air - fire - water and all living things?
Without it - all that exists may be destroyed.

Without respect for the earth -
there is no growth - no plants - no food - no life.
Without respect for water -
no growth - no food - no drink - no life.
Without respect for the air -
no plants - no possibility of breathing - no life.
Without respect for fire and care over its use
we have destruction - a wasteland - no life.

For 'life' to LIVE we need to replace the 'I' with
that all-encompassing 'O'.
The hug which encircles and includes
and gives us - LOVE.
Love for our earth -
Love for all life -
Love for each other - as a brother
And in this an acknowledgement
of the 'Oneness' - of all LIFE.

A LETTER TO GOD:

Dear Power that is All,

The Generating Organising Dynamic, behind and beyond all thought and form, yet within all thought and form,

How could we be so arrogant as to believe that only we have cognisant ability in the whole of your immeasurable Cosmos.

Of necessity perhaps, it seems - for our own progression back to our source -

we must be isolated from our partners on the path.

to grow -

to learn -

to love - for love is all we need to understand -

In this school of hard knocks, until compassion shines through, our part will not improve and 'stardom' is elusive without humility and love;

To be aware of *our* place in your plan is not essential -
for to be aware of *you* within our plan is all we need.

Generating Organising Dynamic, is a description given fitting the word GOD by Katya Walter in her book 'Tao of Chaos'

SPRING COMES TO ALLAN BANK

Written in Wordsworth's Study at Allan Bank, Grasmere, 24th April 2015,

Soft Spring creeps in as stealthily as the mist on the Fell,
Displaying her arrival in a revealing of freshest greens and yellows,
Giving us assurance that the harsh winds of winter are gone.
Cold greys and dark greens are muted
in the glory of young leaves and dancing flowers.
New shoots of grass make the fields a boon
to the hardy, grazing sheep and their new-born lambs
And offer to our hearts a healing.
The white flakes drifting down, that earlier were of lacy snow,
are now those of delicate cherry blossom,
And in the village,
the empty branches unfurl in brighter pinks and reds
as they too compete with our signal call from the house on the hill
- that –"All is well with the world!"

VOICES OF THE PAST

Voices of the past give you their memories and experiences
but they are not yours,
and yours are as valid to you as theirs to them.
They wrote their truth
and as you have often said
it is as a 'religious experience'
- a touching of the light of God
- an awareness of the love
which can encompass you
from those who have gone to the Summerlands.
Sceptics will challenge it, for it is not yet their time
to experience what you know
- feel
- hold to your heart.

"Om mani padme hum!"
May this blessing be with them.

I had received a request to publish a book by a scientific researcher who had never experienced any psychic phenomena and was intending to draw his material from books already published. The title was to be "Life After Death: Should I believe?" As I later sat in meditation I felt I had to write and as I finished writing, I heard this Yogic chant on a music track being played. It invokes the benevolent attention of Chenresing – the Tibetan embodiment of compassion. I did not publish the book.

SO SLIPS YOUR LIFE

Soft silver sand slips silently from your hands.
It slides effortlessly through the hour-glass,
so effortlessly too slips your life through the years.
The times of life cannot be reversed to have another start.
All that time is gone and never returns.
You can have another go at a task
but now it will be from knowledge -
not from the innocent stance you had the first time.
Let the lessons learned
be to your advantage
by listening to that small whisper within.

THANKS BE ...

In friendship people draw together
Sharing thoughts and dreams and love
Thanking those who see our longing
To share in work for those above.

In like minds we join together
To share our love of the spirit folk
To thank those souls who have the patience
To help us, when we decide to work.

Thanks be to God our Divine inspirer
And all our spirit companions dear.
Thank you too for the earthly friendship
Of people who relieve communication's fear.

Though easy 'sacred communion'
May never be my lot
I give thanks for the friendship of spirit
And will work with what I've got.

NO TIME !

Are we considering there is no essence of time passing
therefore there is no urgency or no sense of need
of things to be done?

Or are we saying there is no time left
- but one instant in which to say or do one last act?
To say I love you, hold you, forgive you
or ask forgiveness of you -
What would your last act be and to whom?

But if there is no sense of time - then what?
- in this sphere of no-time-passing
we can spend as long as we like
in attention to something.
But what....?

IT'S A TEAM GAME

These words came out of 'no-where' when I stood to give a philosophical address in a service at a Spiritualist centre near Benidorm in 2004. No previous thought had been given to what I would speak about that evening, and out of the many I have on record I felt it important to include this one here. The final poem had been part of my husband's reading before my address.

Life seems to be a never-ending struggle. Sometimes it is a very nice struggle - you enjoy doing what you are doing and pushing forward. I found a quotation recently in a book by Lynn De Swarte, who was Editor at *Psychic News* for a time and she said:

"Life being a never-ending struggle to achieve love and wisdom, it is better to strive for that here, than to move on as a spiritually deficient individual into other dimensions. Heaven and Hell are conditions of consciousness which can manifest here on earth just as easily as in a future state of existence."

Just think, we can make our own life hell because we worry about things, we are frightened of things–we don't think we can do it–we're not sure if we ought to. Instead of just saying 'Well if you're not sure–go for it; give it a try; give it a whirl!'

Life is really what you make it and the people that you draw into your life as well. They make your life, because of the way that you are towards people and towards your life. You draw towards you the people who fit with your life, and give you pleasure to be with, as you give them pleasure by being with them because it's a team- it's a team-game being here on earth. You can't live totally on your own. I mean you have to go to the shop for a start–you have to get food–you have to go and pay the rates–you have to get about–you have to meet up with people. You have to have people who will respond to you and will negotiate with you - so you learn to play by a set of rules.

If you don't - then everything will be total chaos!

It seems to be at that stage now because people aren't playing by the rules; the people are fighting against each other—they want their way! They don't see that if everybody just gave a little, took a little, gave a little more, it balances, that you then have co-operation and a team game.

We have a chance while we are here to improve our team game and maybe get out of the Second Division or Third Division depending on where you feel are and we might even make it up as far as the Premiership—if we learn to play the game—one by the rules—but also to the best of our ability. By playing the game to the best of our ability, our abilities improve, and we get better and so instead of being way down somewhere—not even in a league, we move up. It is just our response to things, to our way of thinking and knowing too that we are not alone.

We are not alone.

We don't just have the people here around us, on a physical level, that we interact with, are friendly with, help and they help us - we also have a huge team over the other side and of course the Boss himself. If you are in any doubt about something, you just go straight to the Boss, and He can then delegate. Now, I know God won't mind me calling him the Boss, because he is and we are all a part of his team. And if you are stuck, the one thing to do is say a Prayer. By that we ask, and we have a whole team, from the angels to our own much-loved family in the different levels of the whole Universe to come and help us.

They cannot help us if we don't ask. They are not allowed to, because we have FREEWILL and if we want to - we can do it our way.

"I'll do it my way! And I'll make a mess of it" or I can say "Help! I just need a bit of help." Then just stay quiet because it is in those quiet times that our help can come. The little thought that says "I know I can ring so and so'—I know I can just go next door but one. I think they may know the answer."

So, give the chance for that thought to come in, for even when we say 'Oh they don't answer my prayers,' all prayers are answered in some way. But it may just be that little thought that comes in.

You think it is all your idea–well if so, why hadn't you thought of it before. Maybe it is and maybe it is just your own self, because we don't just work on this physical level, we do work on our own higher level that is a bit more in touch with what we are capable of, and in that way we can help ourselves by listening.

Many years ago Dame Julian of Norwich, wrote, "For ten people who say 'Listen Lord I'm speaking.' There is one who says, 'Speak Lord, I am listening.'."

It is in those listening moments, when you have made your quiet prayer, that the help comes–whether it is just the strength to go on another day–whether it is the idea that puts your action on its way–whether it is help for somebody who is in need, they are always there. We are never without our spirit team.

So we have our earthly team to play with, we have our spirit team that we can fall back on, and with all pulling as one we work together for the good of the Universe–for the future–for our future and for our happiness and fulfilment while we are here.

For as Helen Steiner Rice wrote:

"Remember that ideals are like stars in the sky,
You can never really reach them, hanging in the heavens high...
But like the mighty mariner who sailed the storm-tossed sea
And used the stars to chart his course with skill and certainty.
You too can chart your course in life with high ideals and love,
For high ideals are like the stars that light the sky above...
You cannot ever reach them but lift your heart up high
And your life will be as shining as the stars up in the sky."

GO IN PEACE

Go peaceably among the world
and succour give
wherever there is need,
that in your life
it may be said
you followed a Master's creed.

Go gently on the path of truth,
that all who meet thee
shall say – their way
is truly of the light
and their words
are worthy to be heard.

Go placidly amidst the noise
and you shall see the sun
that warms your days,
and the moon that shares vour
dreams,
in full reality.

Go in Peace.

CPSIA information can be obtained
at www.ICGtesting.com
Printed in the USA
BVHW070030130223
658293BV00014B/1646

9 781908 421371